" The stars are always shining, so is my love for you.
Look up sweet love! The stars shine through. " Isabel K.T.

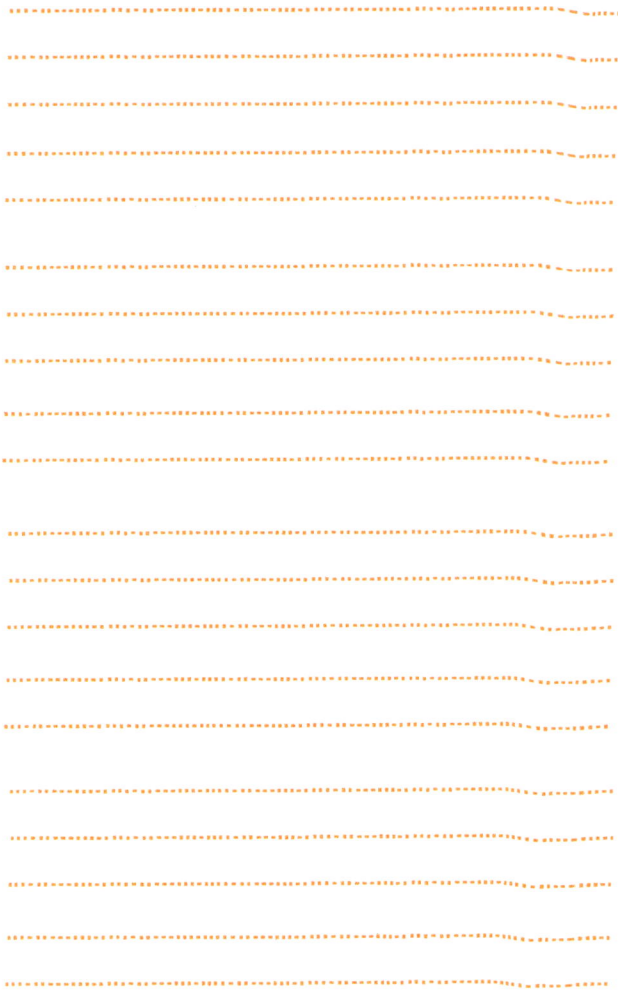

"A bright balloon can inspire wonder,
a walk with you forever." Isabel K. T.

"Loving You Is Forever Sunshine." Isabel K.T.

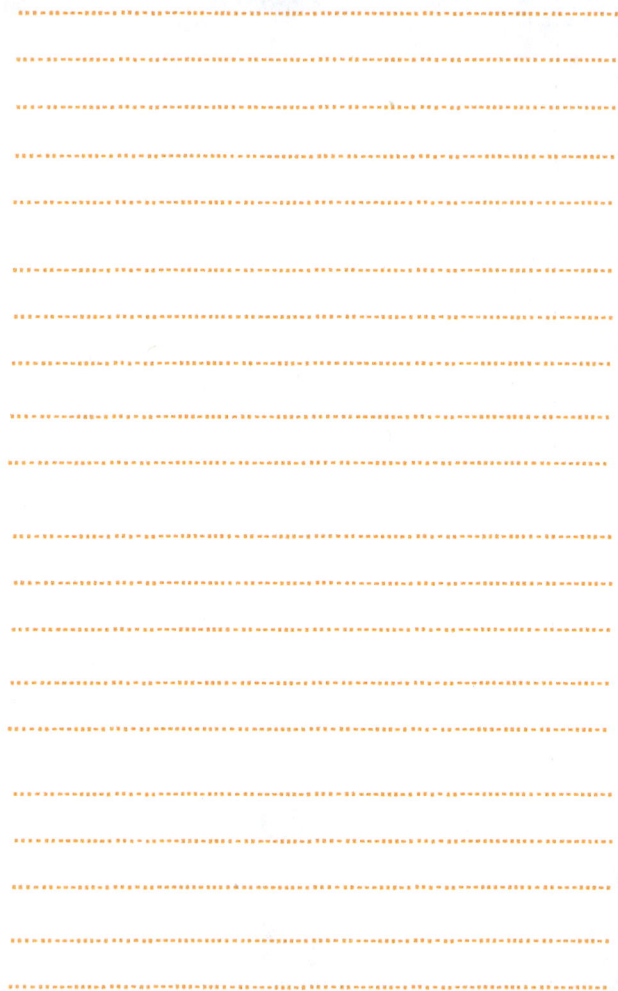

"When dream and reality coincide,
in perfect harmony love resides." Isabel K. T.

"Love four me is you" Isabel K. T.

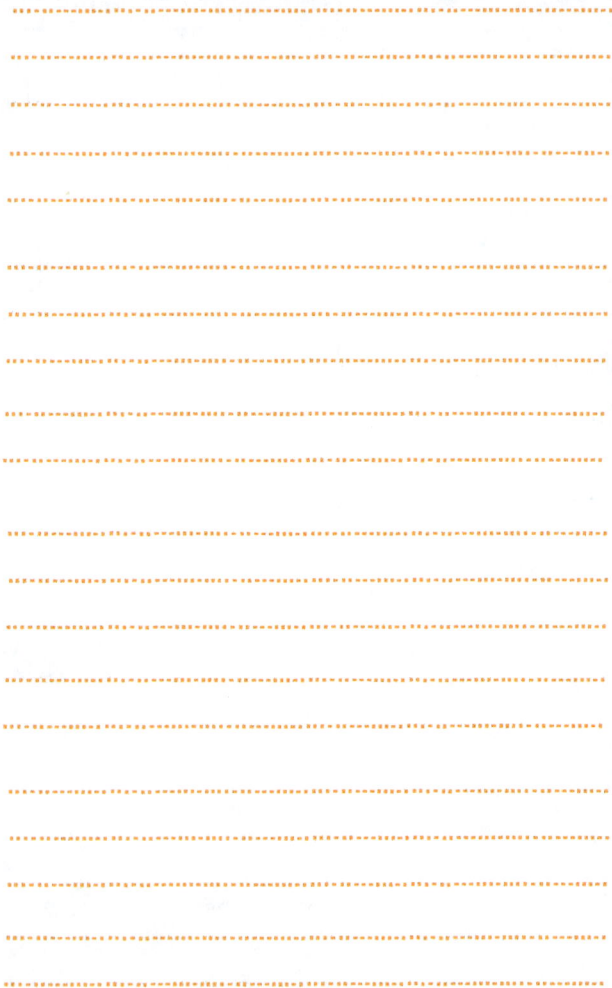

"Can we stay longer just to expand forever?
Loving you springs eternal!" Isabel K.T.

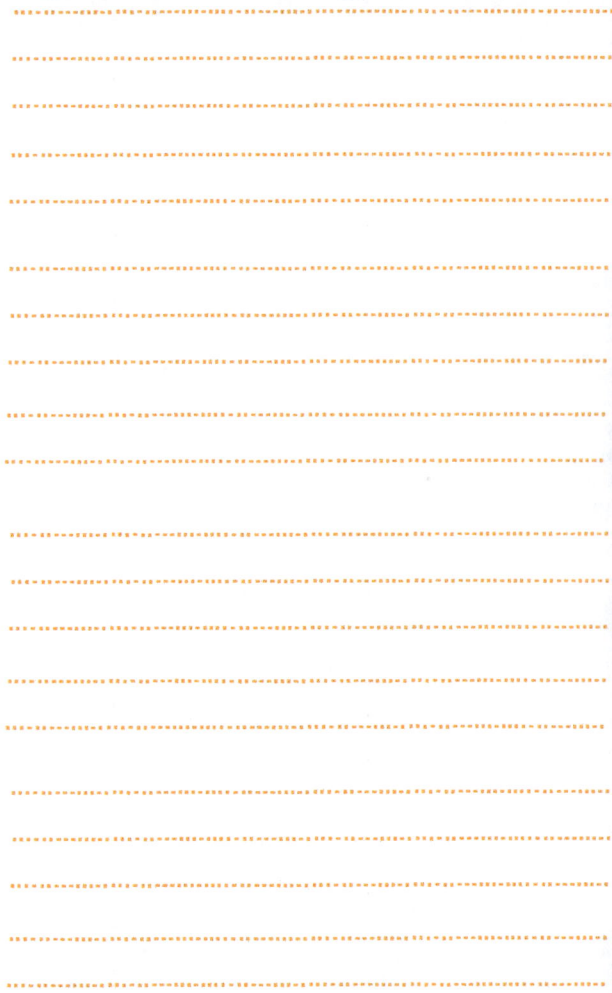

"I know you & I love you.
That is all I need to know." Isabel K T

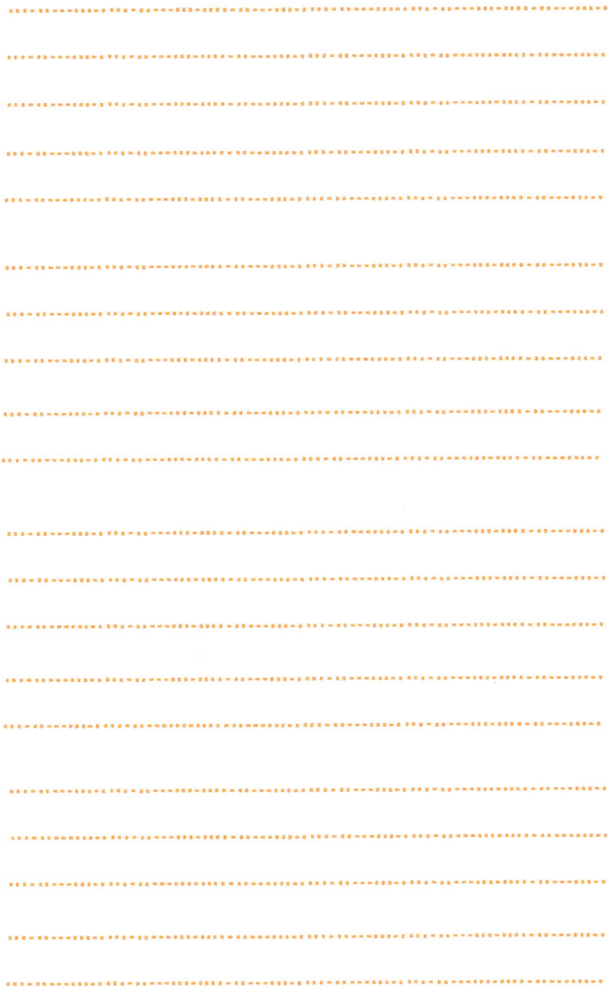

"Heart, I'm here, loving you eternal." Isabel K.T.

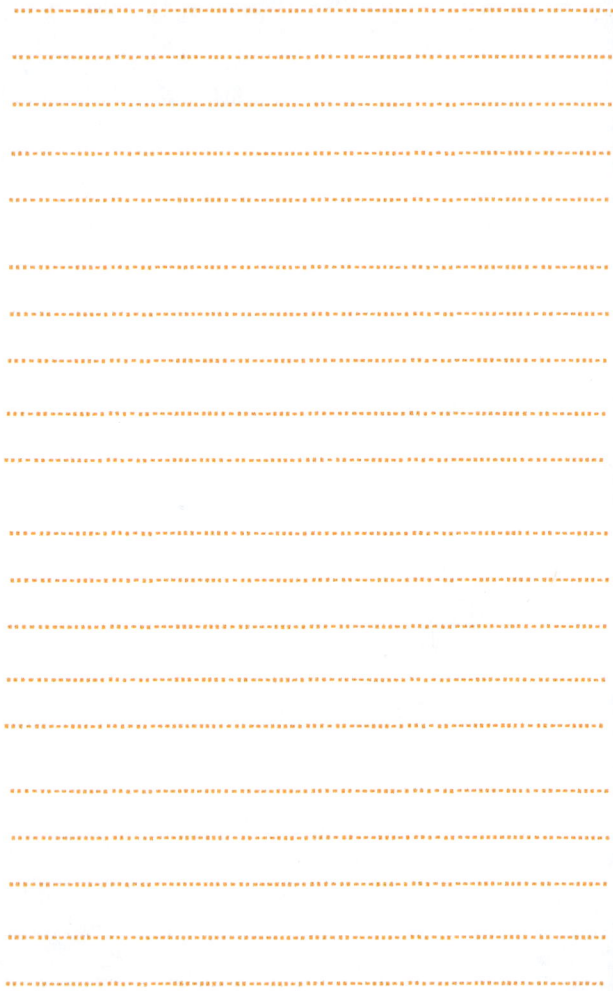

"I will only let the stars deliver the message I cannot, for I trust their light to find you and blessedly bring you my love." Isabel K. T.

"Heart, sweet blessing,
now the stars know the truth too."
Isabel K. T

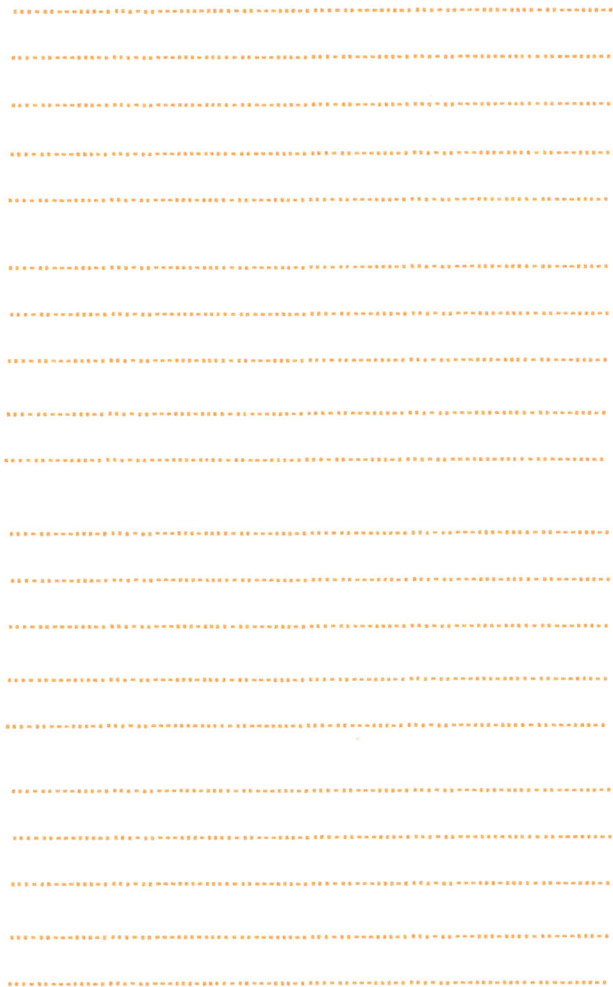

"Gentle, loving, light, loving you is my delight,
& into it I happily lean
for life with you is a welcome dream." Isabel K. T.

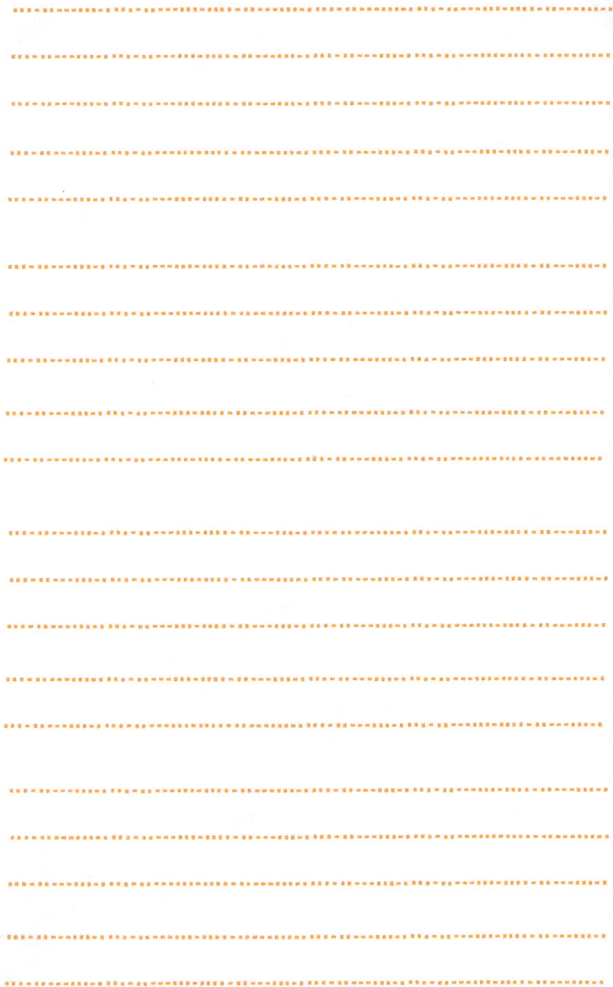

"My sole has met it's match, and now is dancing in the stars to
write 'I LOVE YOU.'" Isabel R.T

"A loving heart says 'I love you,' & my heart dances to its
rhythm so that in silence you can hear it too." Isabel K.T.

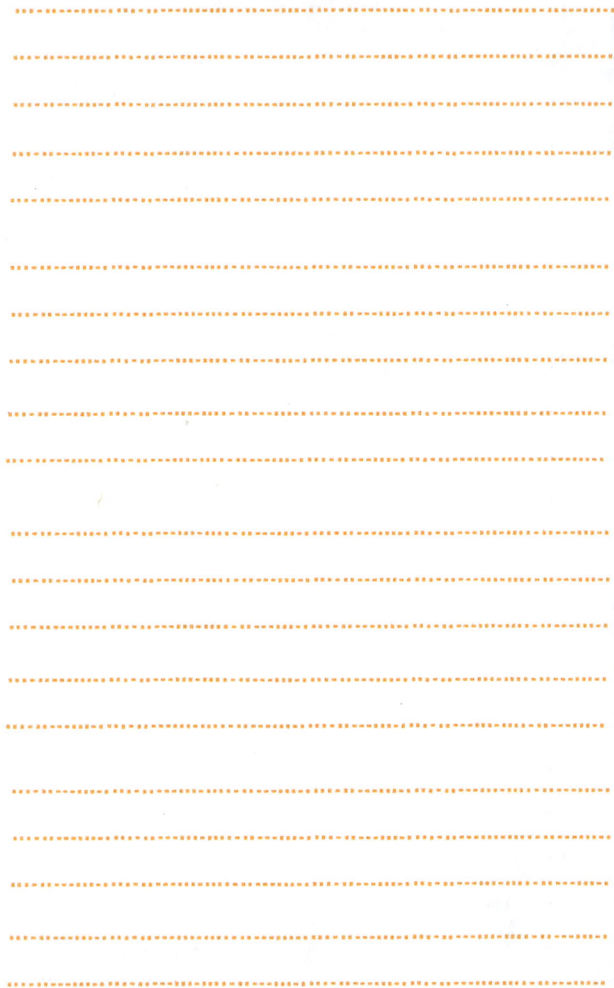

"One Morning I woke up & the sun was saying your name. I
asked the stars if they do for you the same — and so they
helped me say what my heart longed to, a gentle & all lasting:
I LOVE YOU." Isabel K.T.

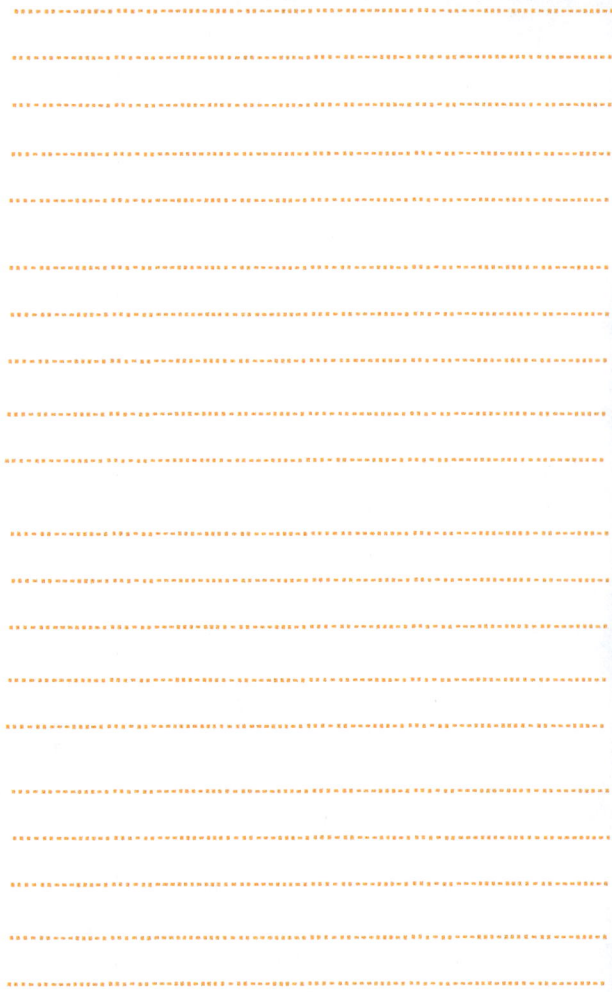

"I Love You." Isabel K.T.

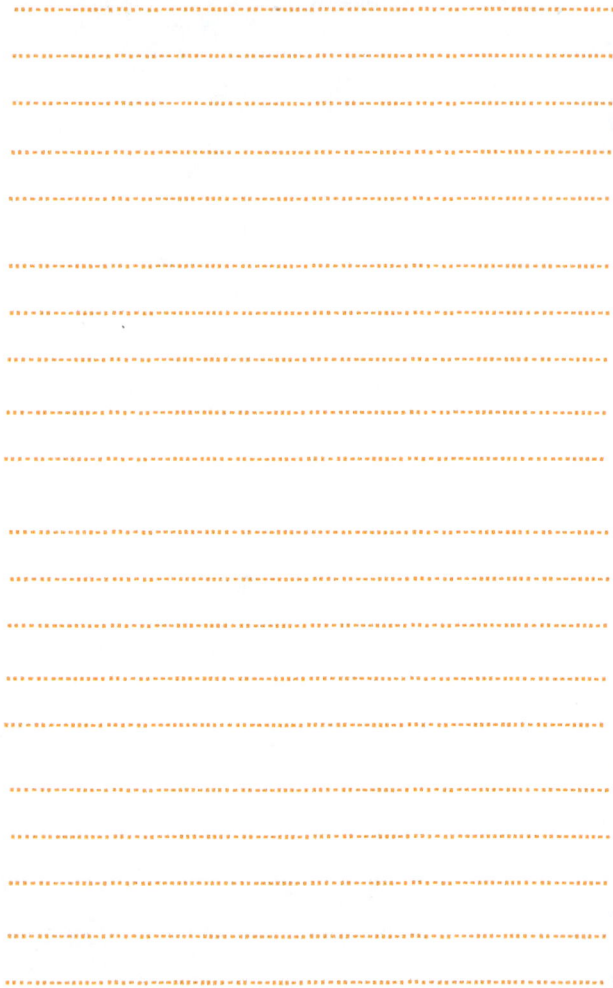

"Loving you is the most natural essence of my life." Isabel K. T.

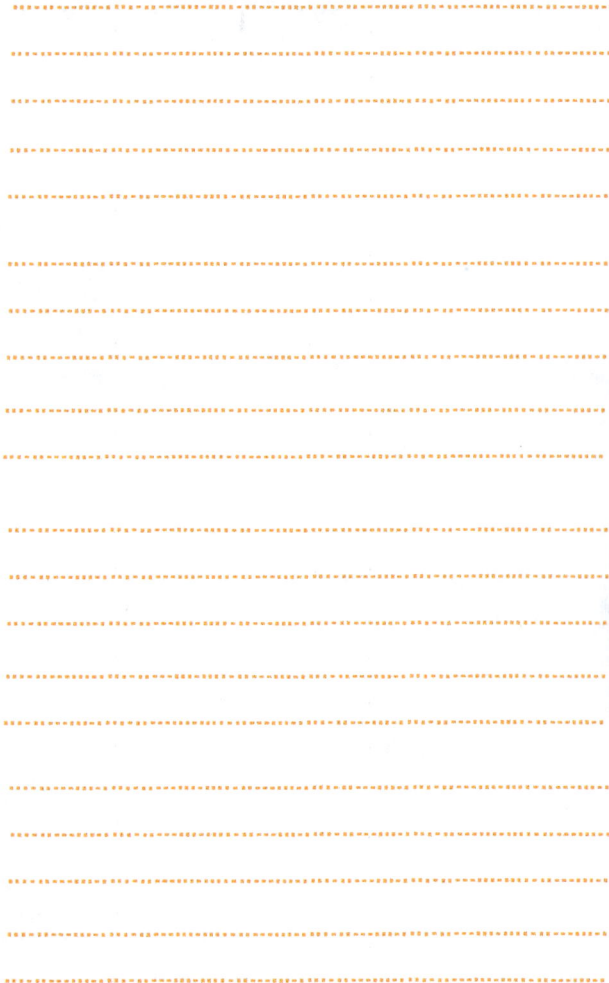

"Amarte es una bendición." Isabel K.T.

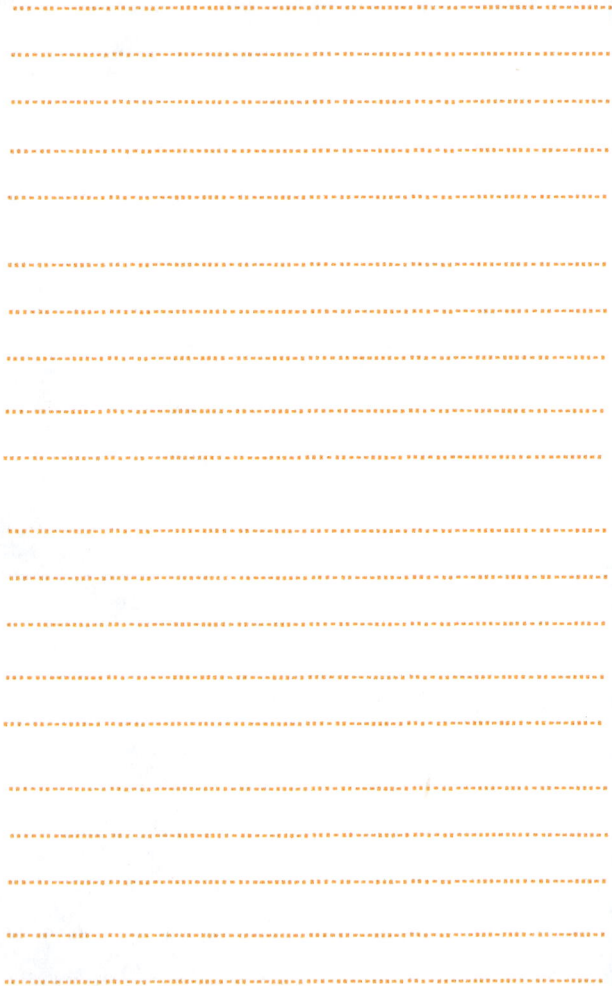

"Peppering the skies with joyful meaning,
now the stars celebrate your wonder with me." Isabel K.T.

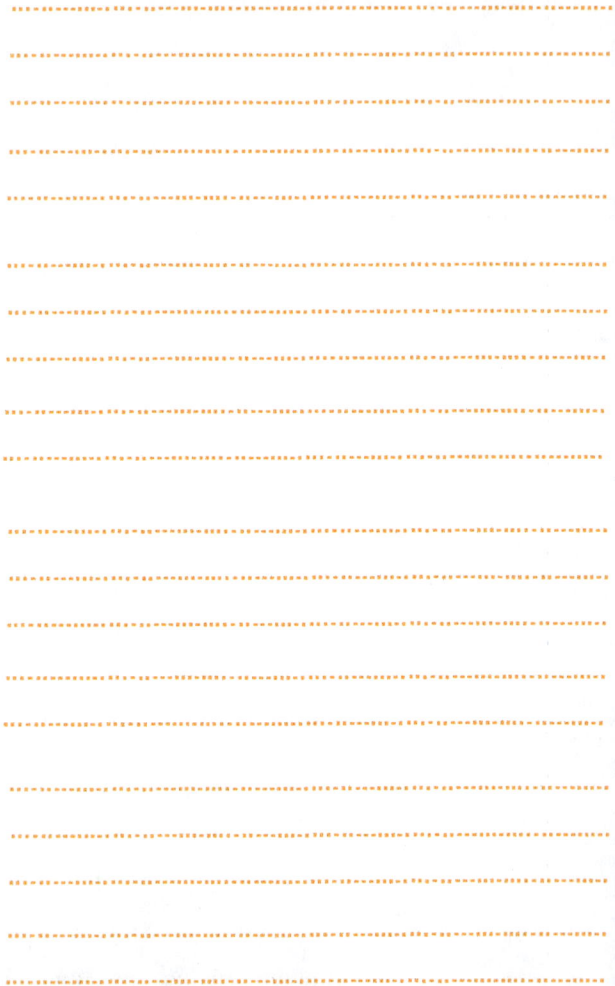

"When I look up at the sky I see wonder & heaven together."
Isabel K.T.

"My universe expands to love you more dear heart!" Isabel K. T.

"Upon seeing you far away, I had to dream a dream, and in it's
wings I found the truth, that love's eternal shine, is true & in
that truth (you) divine." Isabel K.T.

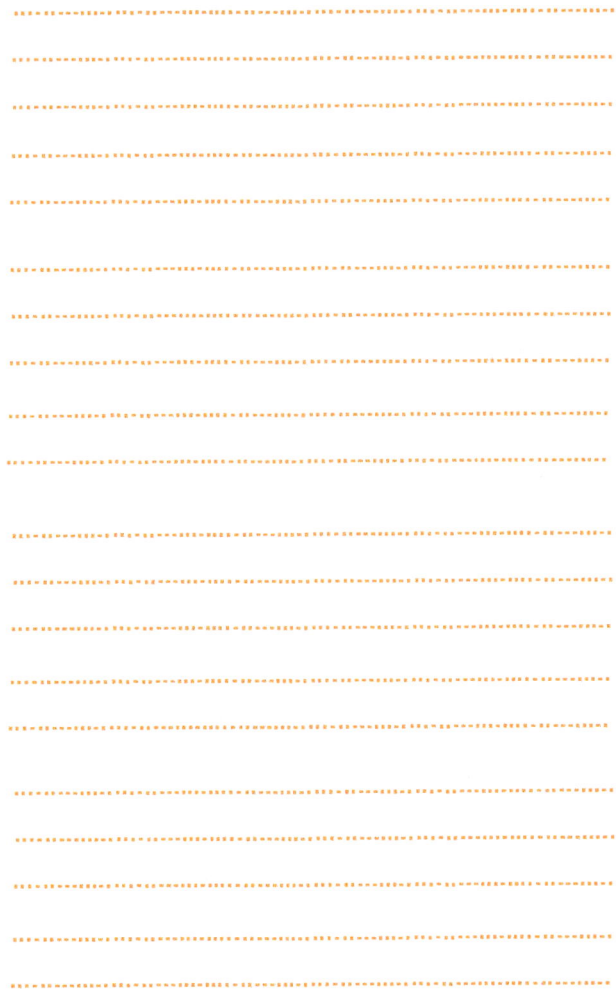

'Star sailor look up, the stars shine bright and brighter for you.
for in them I wrote your way home dear heart in a bright road –
I LOVE YOU.'
Isabel K.T.

"A heart leads the way, a compass that knows true north, &
always finds what it seeks." Isabel K.T.

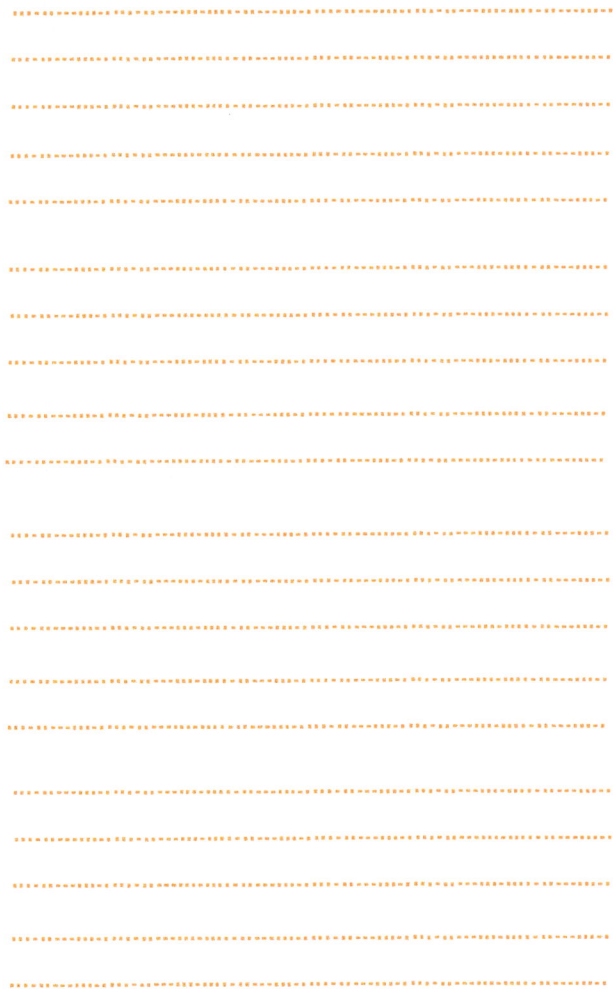

"One night at a time, One day in the distance,
Forever in harmonious bliss,
stars shine on & on into a new existence."
Isabel K. T.

" Three letters turn to one, three words one emotion, time in
perpetuity — u, love, always." Isabel K.T.

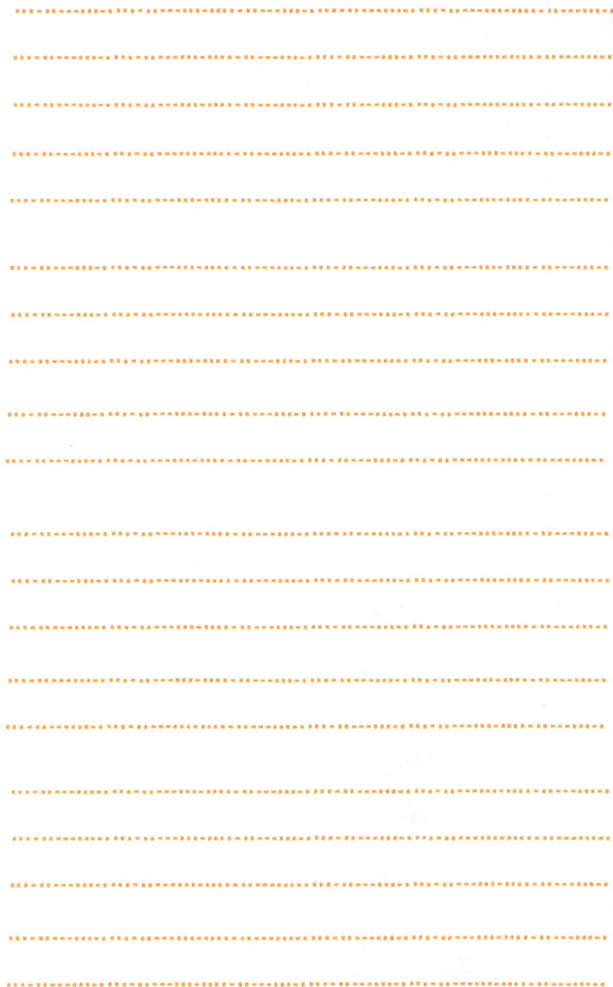

"Love shines brightly from the heart, look up, the stars are shinning brightly too, you do the math, my answer (always) is 'I LOVE YOU'." Isabel K.T

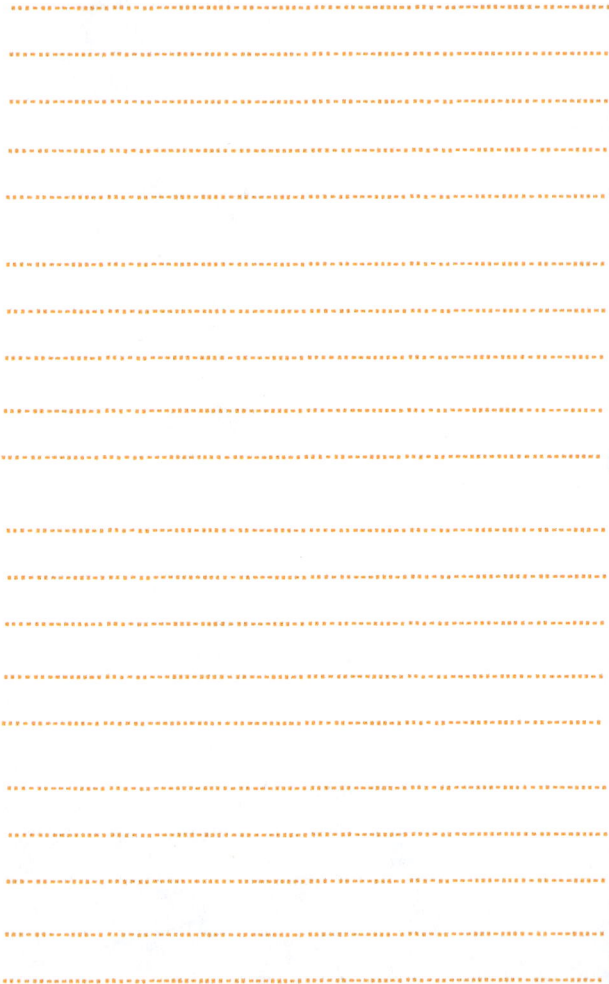

"Peachy are the cheeks filled with good health & memories of love." Isabel K.T.

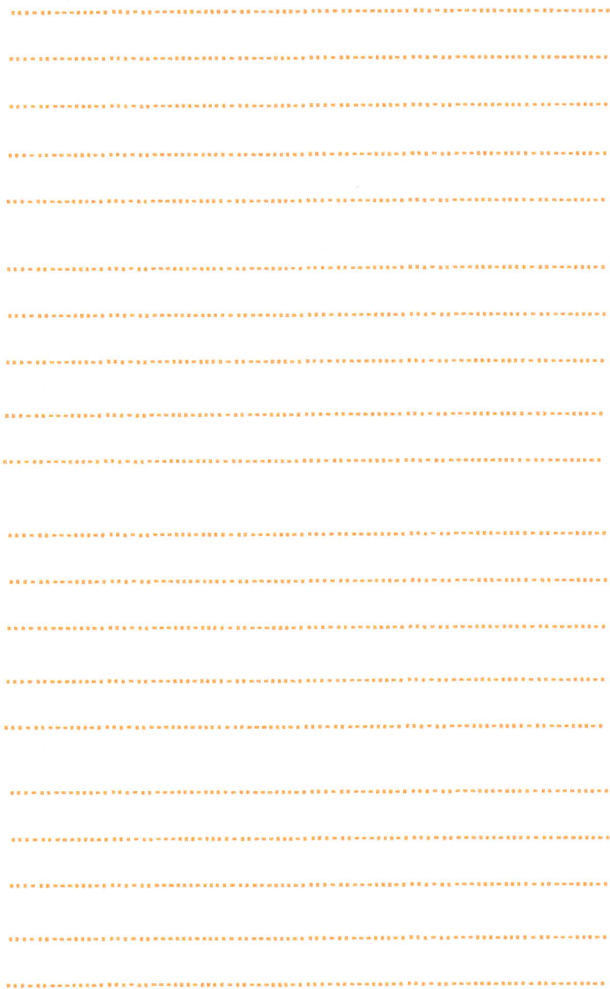

"I'm dancing in the stars just to write you a love note, so when
you look up you see, you were always the love for me."
Isabel K.T.

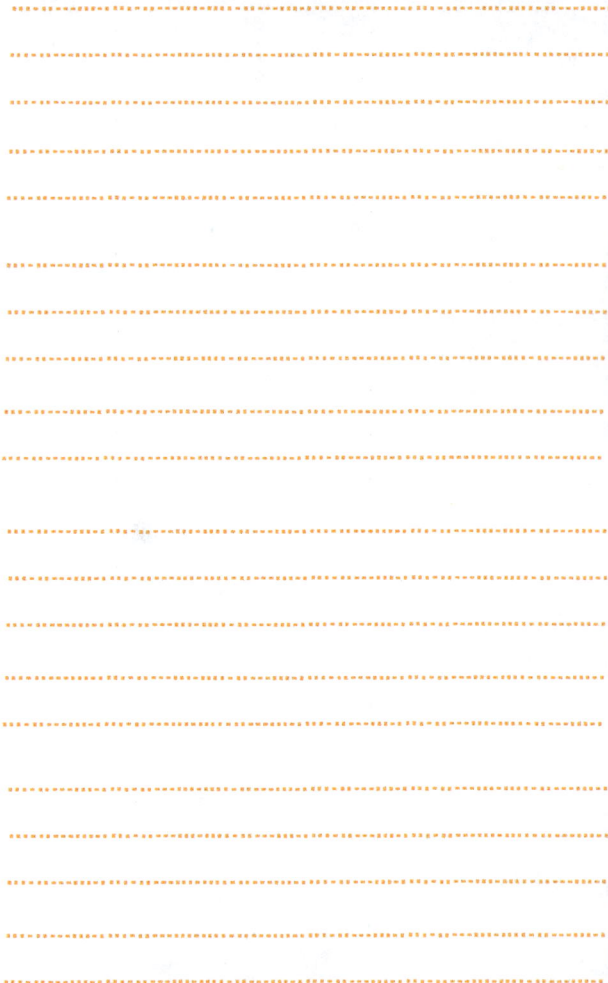

"A loving thought, a sweet caress, a tender embrace,
love does the rest." Isabel K.T.

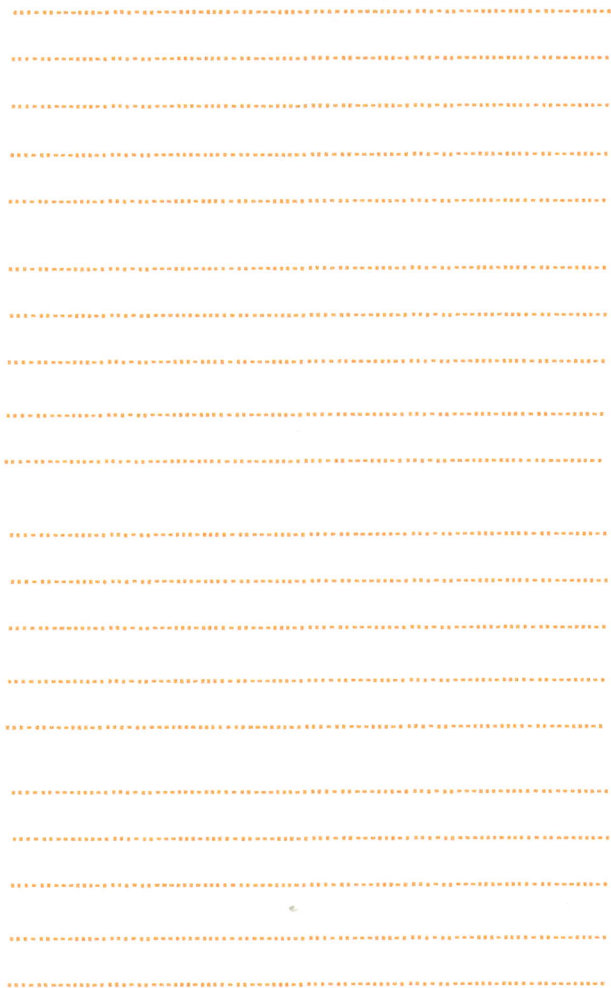

"Every night I make a wish, that love's true light gives you my kiss, & dear heart I know it's true, for your cheek is flushed with my 'I Love You.'" Isabel K.T.

"A loving moment shared is forever remembered." Isabel K.T.

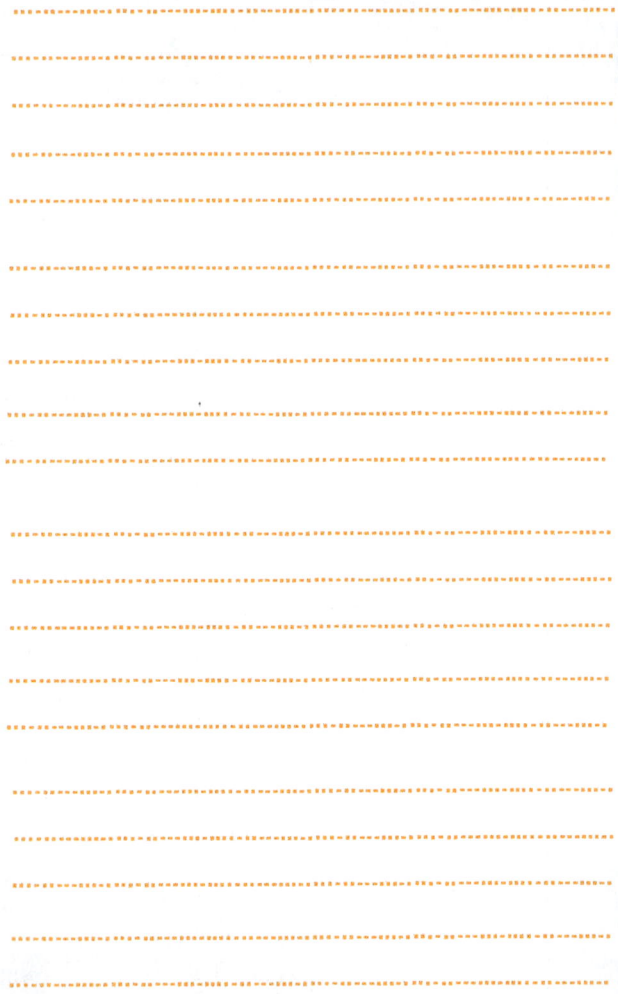

"Shine bright beautiful angel, you are made of stardust,
dress up with the best of you." Isabel K.T.

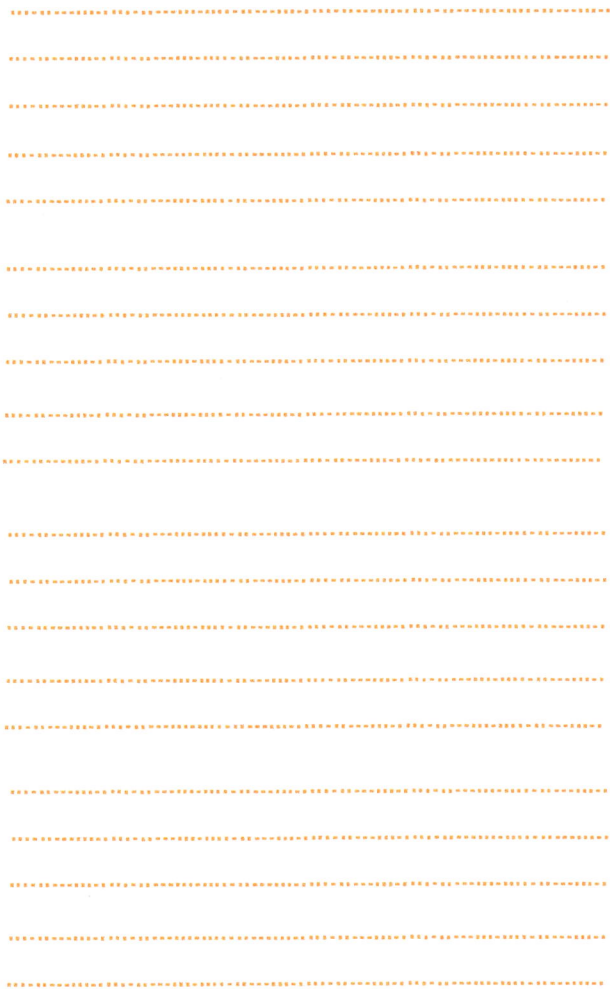

"I saw a star moving across the night sky, and I remembered if
stars can move, so can I, hold fast dear heart – i am on my way
home." Isabel K. T.

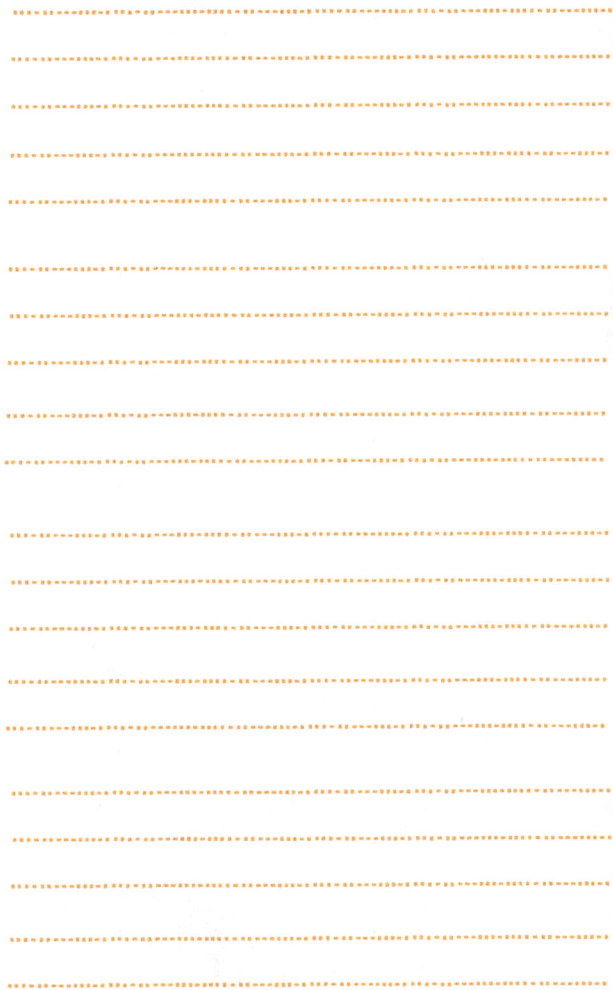

"The moon is smiling bright, the stars are telling it it's true, the
love it sees at night, stays by daylight too." Isabel K. T.

'The stars are dancing, they shine brightly all day long, even when we cannot see them, if we close our eyes we hear their song — Look Up!' Isabel K.T.

"For love, the odds are always favorable, to love is the only
journey we truly need to make." Isabel K.T.

"Loving you is easy, loving you is wonderful, loving you is all I
need to now that dreams come true." Isabel K.T.

"All you need is love, and love is all you need, why darling when it comes from me to you, it is a love that's guaranteed."
Isabel K.T.

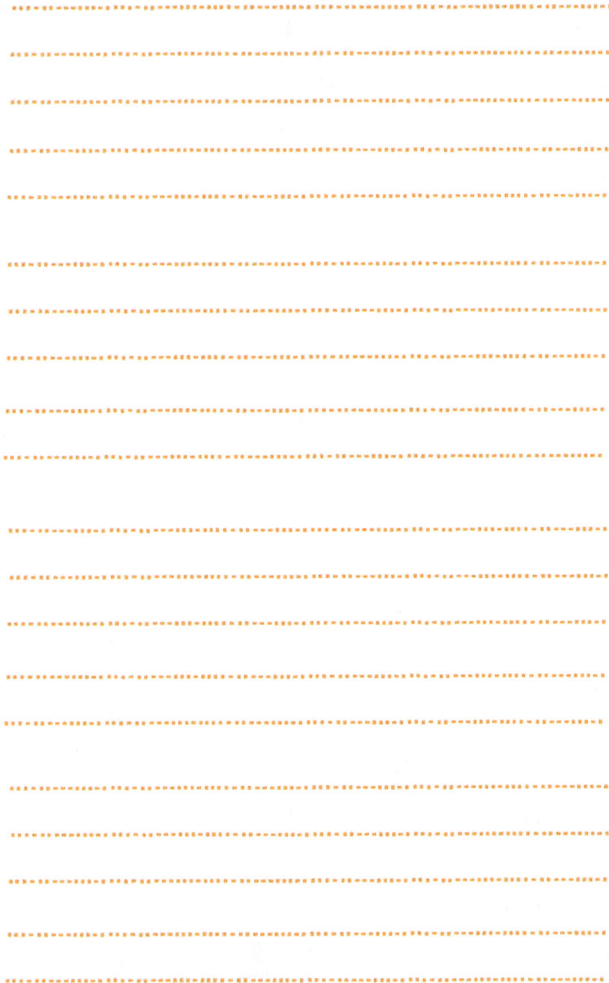

"My heart is beating 'I Love You' can you hear it?
It dances to the light in your smile." Isabel K.T.

"Every journey knows the stars will guide you safely home,
you just have to 'look up'." Isabel K.T.

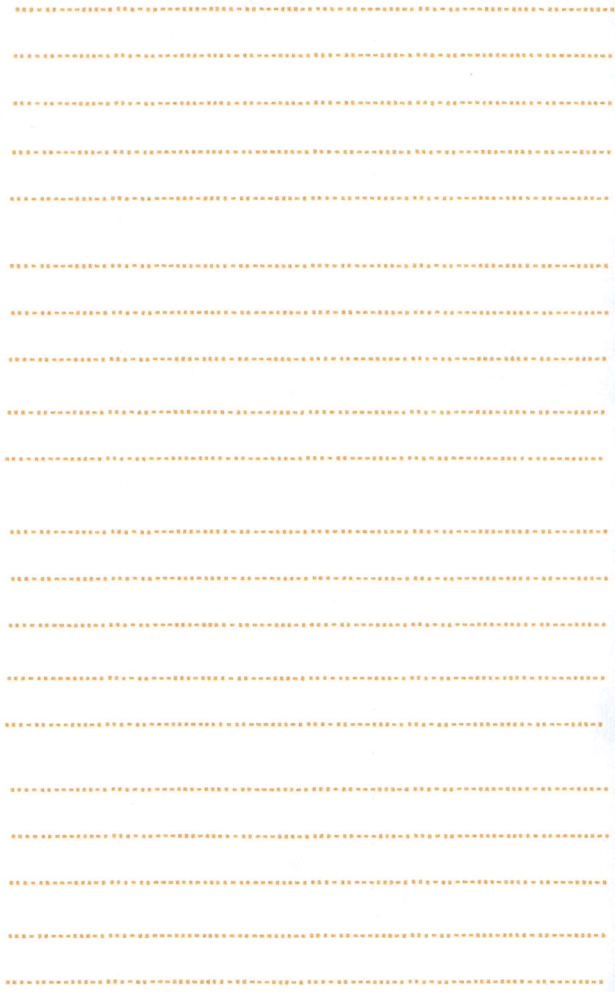

"I love you say the stars, & I couldn't agree more,
I love you day and night. Four what's not to adore,
your heart is delightfully everything & I get to love it more.
In case you are still wondering, dear heart I'm forever yours."
Isabel K.T.

"Look Up, the sky shines bright,
Look Up they stars do too.
Look Up & you will find,
That when you are far away,
They always help me say
What my heart most wants to..
"I   LOVE   YOU'." Isabel K. T

"For my dear heart — always"

www.ingramcontent.com/pod-product-compliance
Lightning Source LLC
Chambersburg PA
CBHW062134040426
42335CB00039B/2110